School Crossing Guards

by Terri DeGezelle

Consultant:
Laura Wilkinson
Community Division
National Safety Council

Bridgestone Books
an imprint of Capstone Press
Mankato, Minnesota

Bridgestone Books are published by Capstone Press
151 Good Counsel Drive, P.O. Box 669, Mankato, Minnesota 56002
http://www.capstone-press.com

Library of Congress Cataloging-in-Publication Data
DeGezelle, Terri, 1955–
    School crossing guards/by Terri DeGezelle.
    p.cm.—(Community helpers)
    Includes bibliographical references and index.
    ISBN 0-7368-0959-7
    1. School crossing guards—Juvenile literature. [1. School crossing guards.] I. Title.
II. Community helpers (Mankato, Minn.)
LB2865 .D38 2002
363.12′57—dc21   00-012546

Summary: A simple introduction to the work school crossing guards do, the tools they use,
    the clothing they wear, and their importance to the communities they serve.

Editorial Credits
Sarah Lynn Schuette, editor; Karen Risch, product planning editor; Linda Clavel,
    cover designer; Heidi Schoof, photo researcher

Photo Credits
Bob Daemmrich/Pictor, 10
Capstone Press/Gary Sundermeyer, 12
David F. Clobes, Stock Photography, 4, 16
Photri-Microstock, cover
Shaffer Photography/James L. Shaffer, 6, 8, 20
Unicorn Stock Photos/Alice M. Prescott, 14; Martin R. Jones, 18

1 2 3 4 5 6 07 06 05 04 03 02

Table of Contents

School Crossing Guards

School crossing guards help children who walk to and from school. They stop cars at intersections. School crossing guards help children cross streets safely.

intersection
a place where two streets or roads meet and cross each other

What School Crossing Guards Do

School crossing guards stand near sidewalks and in crosswalks. They hold out orange flags or stop signs to stop cars. School crossing guards then tell children to cross the street.

Where Crossing Guards Work

School crossing guards work at busy intersections near schools. Other crossing guards work at railroad crossings and construction sites. These crossing guards help keep dangerous places safe for people who walk.

Tools School Crossing Guards Use

School crossing guards carry flags, stop signs, and whistles. They use flags and stop signs to stop cars. School crossing guards sometimes blow whistles to direct traffic.

traffic
moving cars and trucks on streets, roads, and highways

What School Crossing Guards Wear

Most school crossing guards wear bright safety vests or rain coats. The bright colors help drivers see school crossing guards. School crossing guards often wear warm hats, boots, and gloves in cold weather.

Types of School Crossing Guards

Many school crossing guards are paid for their work. Other school crossing guards are volunteers. Some schools have school patrollers. These older students help younger students cross the street.

volunteer
someone who offers to do a job without pay

15

How School Crossing Guards Learn

School crossing guards learn safety rules from police officers. School patrollers sometimes go to safety camp. School crossing guards and school patrollers learn how to stop and start traffic correctly.

People Who Help Crossing Guards

Police officers teach traffic rules to school crossing guards. They also help direct busy traffic. Teachers, parents, and police officers teach students to cross the street safely.

How Crossing Guards Help Others

School crossing guards help children walk to and from school safely. They help drivers see children and other people who walk. School crossing guards keep streets safe for children.

Hands On: Walk Safely

School crossing guards help people cross the street safely. Listen to your school crossing guard or school patroller. They will tell you when it is safe to cross the street. But every intersection does not have a crossing guard. You can learn to walk safely by following the tips below.

1. Always cross the street at an intersection or a crosswalk.
2. Stop at the curb or edge of the street.
3. Look left, right, and left again before crossing the street.
4. Keep looking for traffic as you cross the street.
5. Follow all traffic signs. Ask your parents to explain what the signs mean.
6. Try to walk with your parents, with a friend, or in a group.
7. Wear bright clothes so drivers can see you better.
8. Never run when crossing the street.

Words to Know

intersection (IN-tur-sek-shuhn)—a place where two streets or roads meet and cross each other; school crossing guards usually stand at intersections.

traffic (TRAF-ik)—moving cars and trucks on streets, roads, and highways; school crossing guards sometimes direct traffic.

volunteer (vol-uhn-TIHR)—someone who offers to do a job without pay; many school crossing guards are volunteers.

Read More

Mattern, Joanne. *Safety at School.* Safety First. Edina, Minn.: Abdo, 1999.

Ready, Dee. *School Bus Drivers.* Community Helpers. Mankato, Minn.: Bridgestone Books, 1998.

Internet Sites

Pedestrian Safety
http://www.nhtsa.dot.gov/kids/biketour/pedsafety/index.html

Stay Alert, Stay Safe
http://www.sass.ca/kmenu.htm

Index